GUIDELINES FOR RELIGIOUS EDUCATION

3.

HEIRS TO THE KINGDOM

CATECHESIS FOR CHILDREN: Infancy to Pre-Adolescence

by
Nora Hanlon

St Paul Publications

St Paul Publications
Middlegreen, Slough SL3 6BT

Nihil obstat: Francis Leonard
Imprimatur: † David Konstant
Bishop in Central London
5th June 1980.

First published July 1980.
Printed in Great Britain by the Society of St Paul, Slough.
ISBN 0 85439 177 0

St Paul Publications is an activity of the priests and brothers of the Society of St Paul who promote the christian message through the mass media.

CONTENTS

REFERENCES

DOCUMENTS OF VATICAN II

ALP	Decree on the Apostolate of Lay People
CSL	Constitution on the Sacred Liturgy
DCC	Dogmatic Constitution on the Church
DCDR	Dogmatic Constitution on Divine Revelation
DCE	Declaration on Christian Education
DCMA	Decree on the Church's Missionary Activity

SUBSEQUENT DOCUMENTS

CS	The Catholic School, The Sacred Congregation for Christian Education, CTS
CT	Catechesis in Our Time, Apostolic Exhortation of Pope John Paul II, St Paul Publications, CTS
DCM	Directory on Children's Masses, Sacred Congregation for Divine Worship, CTS
GCD	General Catechetical Directory, Sacred Congregation for the Clergy, CTS
TFNW	Teaching the Faith the New Way, The Bishops' Conference of England and Wales, St Paul Publications

PART ONE

1.

Principles

(cf. Cornerstone: 6-9; 17; 25-33; 41-54; 57-58; 119-123; 200-205; 210-211; 216-221)

Implications of Baptism

1. The liturgy of the new Rite of Baptism for Children presents us with a dramatic picture from which it is possible to draw direct conclusions for the future catechesis of the child who lies unknowing in his mother's arms. The child, the chief actor in the drama, is passive and so the invitations, exhortations and the requests are addressed, in the first instance, to the parents who present their new-born infant. Here we have the local Church, ideally as the worshipping Church assembled for the Eucharist, gathered to welcome this new member. The priest is the authoritative spokesman and minister for the community. The parents who have given life to the child, now seek to prepare him for eternal life. Here, at the font, is the beginning of this privileged relationship with the Trinity which will grow throughout his earthly life, if it is fostered by those into whose care God has entrusted his natural well-being. So the godparents especially and the rest of the "faith"-ful present, undertake that by word and example they will assist the parents in nurturing the child until he reaches the stage of maturity when he can recognise that he has "put on" Christ and accept for himself the privileges and responsibilities of christian commitment.

2. The message is clear. It is the child who is baptised and anointed for it is the child who has been chosen for the dignity of a son of God. But just as the child cannot reach full human maturity without the help of the adults in his environment, so too, his spiritual maturity is dependent upon them.

This is why the parents are instructed before the baptism of a child, so that they will have time to consider and understand the grave responsibility they undertake. This is why, also, since Vatican II great stress has been laid on adult christian education and why the *General Catechetical Directory* urges bishops to "remember that catechesis for adults, since it deals with persons who are capable of an adherence that is fully responsible, must be considered the chief form of catechesis. All the other forms, which are indeed always necessary, are in some way oriented to it".[1] While no man can set limits upon the action of the Holy Spirit, the Bishops' Conference of England and Wales in *Teaching the Faith the New Way* point out that without catechesis "the man would grow, but the Christian in him would not grow" for it is the mature christian adults who "then become the educators and the catechists of the new christian generations. In the world of today, pluralist and secularised as it is, the Church bears witness to its hope[2] in the measure of the maturity in faith of its adult members".[3]

If the child, then, is to grow in faith, it will be as a result of the combined action of those present when he first receives the gift: the parents, who are "the first to pass on the faith to their children and to educate them in it"[4] and the local Church in which the child will spend his early years. Here we have the reason why the parish provides its Catholic school which "enables young people, while developing their own personality, to grow at the same time in that new life which has been given them in baptism".[5] A successful catechesis for children, therefore, will arise out of the cooperation of parents, school and parish. In so far as the three elements work together for the christian education of the child, he will be enabled to become committed to Christ and integrated into the life of his Body, the Church. If they fail, he may enter the adult world fully equipped technologically and in human culture, but with his religious understanding and practice remaining that of a child. It will be a little wonder if he lapses.

Each of the three has its own specific function in that catechesis which is aimed at producing "the believer, the formed and educated Catholic . . . one who has made a free and reflective commitment to Christ in the Church".[6]

Catechesis in the Family

3. To the parents falls the primary duty of nurture in the faith. At the very start of the baptismal ceremony the priest calls upon the parents to recognise the seriousness and importance of what they undertake. "You have asked for your child to be baptised. In doing so you are accepting the responsibility of training him (her) in the practice of the faith". Then briefly he indicates what this involves. Immediately before the actual baptism, the priest re-emphasises the parental responsibility: "On your part, you must make it your constant care to bring him (her) up in the practice of the faith". As he blesses the father almost at the end of the baptismal ceremony, the priest prays that "he and his wife will be the first teachers of the child in the ways of faith. May they be also the best of teachers bearing witness to the faith by what they say and do".[7] Parents do, indeed, pass on their faith by what they are — what they say and do. They teach, bear witness to their faith all the time, but without syllabus or lessons. This teaching is indirect and powerful, born of comments, reactions, enthusiasm for what they see to be "good". They cannot repudiate this duty, nor can they hand it over to the school: "Having chosen it (the school) does not relieve them of a personal duty to give their children a christian upbringing. They are bound to cooperate actively with the school . . . in order to make certain that the school remains faithful to christian principles of education".[8]

The Function of the School in Catechesis

4. Earlier in the same document the specific mission of the school is defined as "a critical, systematic transmission of culture in the light of faith and bringing forth of the power of christian virtue by the integration of culture with faith and of faith with living".[9] Then it is made clear that although the teaching of religion in schools is not confined to the formal lessons in religion, such formal teaching must "be imparted explicitly and in a systematic manner to prevent a distortion in the child's mind between general and religious culture. The fundamental difference between religious

and other forms of education is that its aim is not simply intellectual assent to religious truths but also a total commitment to the Person of Christ".[10]

The Role of the Parish

5. The essential supportive role of the parish community is stated briefly by the priest, as the white garment, "the outward sign of christian dignity", is put on the newly-baptised child. The infant Christian is urged: "With your family and friends to help you by word and example, bring that dignity unstained into the everlasting life of heaven".[11] Discussing the distribution of responsibilities for catechesis the *General Catechetical Directory* speaks of the parish, stating that: "Care must be taken to make the christian community every day conscious of its duty, which is to be a sign of the wisdom and love of God that was revealed to us in Christ".[12]

Integration of Catechesis

6. While each of the three participants in the formation of the growing Christian has its own specific task, it is obvious that there is considerable overlap and this is particularly true in the years of childhood. The catechesis of children is, indeed, a whole which, because of the very nature of childhood, cannot be separated off into sections. Unless there is unanimity of aim, unless each appreciates and supports the role of the other, the child will be confused and, not having yet reached the stage of maturity for free choice, may simply please whoever gives the dominant lead at the moment and in the end, might well repudiate the gift of baptismal faith.

Nature of Catechesis

7. Before considering directly the catechesis of children it would be well to be exact about what is meant. "Catechesis is intended for those who have made, even implicitly, the fundamental choice of Christ and the Church".[13] We are not directly considering the general religious education of a child which can take place outside the community of faith and frequently does, as for example in the good State School. For the Catholic child catechesis falls within his religious education and can be synonymous with it. In all cases, to be lastingly effective it must be at least of the same quality as his general education and always educationally sound. Here we are thinking of the transmission of faith from believer to believer, the passing on to the next generation by a community of believers their beliefs, their attitudes towards these beliefs, the reasons for their beliefs and the living worship which results. It is noteworthy that the Sacred Congregation for the Clergy spends some considerable time discussing the difficulties of such catechesis in the world of today before setting out to define principles and content.[14] Parents and teachers, therefore, while being fully aware of the problems of catechesis, should not be disheartened but rather remember that they have an almighty ally, for the baptised child is a temple of the Holy Spirit.[15] If the environment is smothering "the flame of faith" (prayer at the receiving of the lighted candle), the catechist needs to foster the growth of existing faith, however weakly the spark may flicker.

Indoctrination

8. However, because the child must grow and eventually live in a world which disregards christian life and values, if the catechesis is degraded to become indoctrination, it will, of necessity, be counter-productive. Indoctrination attempts to destroy the freedom of the human person; it tries to enforce, to over-ride, to ignore the freedom of the sons of God.[16] To believe, to be committed to Christ, can only be a free choice, so even from the earliest years the catechist is striving to enable this choice to be made freely. Such a choice cannot be made in childhood, for there is neither the experience nor the maturity required. However, during childhood and adolescence, inadequate, ill-judged, inappropriate, or uninspired catechesis may destroy the possibility of future commitment, of "a free response in Christ and a free adherence to God's initiative".[17] If the faith of the child is not nurtured during childhood, if the child does not know of God's initiative, if Christ is not known and loved, how in mature years can he freely choose commitment? No one expects an eleven-year-old to have the experience to make major choices: to decide which is the best school to meet his needs; where he would choose to live. Those choices are made for him in most spheres of his life for he is still at the stage when nurture is appropriate. In this vital area of faith, nurture is essential to enable him later to be truly free.

To nurture is not to indoctrinate. To nurture is to foster, to guide, to ensure growth. The kind of catechesis appropriate to childhood differs from that of adolescence. In adolescence the wise parent, as also the competent educator, is working towards the point of maturity when he will no longer be required, for his work is complete. Gradually, during adolescence the guiding-reins are released, as greater freedom is given. This cannot be so during childhood. Unless the child lives within an atmosphere of faith, learns the christian way of life in precisely the same way as he learns, for example, the English way of life, or the farming way of life — that is, by living it — he cannot be free to choose or repudiate when his way of life becomes his own to decide. Freedom of choice means that the alternatives are presented. Certainly in these days of instant communication and overt as well as hidden pressure by the media "the kingdom of this world" will be adequately presented. The educator needs to ensure that when the time of choice comes the other alternative is presented at least as effectively. Speaking of adult Christians and their continuing need for catechesis, Pope John Paul II reminds us that "We live in a difficult world in which . . . catechesis should help Christians to be, for their own joy and the service of all, "light" and "salt". Undoubtedly this demands that catechesis should strengthen them in their identity and that it should continually separate itself from the surrounding atmosphere of hesitation, uncertainty and insipidity".[18] He had already discussed "the special characteristics that catechesis assumes at different stages of life",[19] pointing out that during infant years "the child's faculties are integrated into a living relationship with God. It is a work of prime importance. It demands great love and profound respect for the child who has a right to a simple and true presentation of the faith".[20] The catechesis of childhood "communicates to the child the joy of being a witness to Christ in ordinary life".[21] Catechesis which is educationally sound effects this, for " . . . true education is perfectly possible within a tradition of faith. To put the matter in a nutshell: indoctrination is wrong. But indoctrination does not consist in teaching beliefs. It consists in the manner in which and the purpose for which it is done".[22]

"Catechesis thus prepares for the important christian commitment of adult life . . . From infancy until the threshold of maturity, catechesis is thus a permanent school of the faith and follows the major stages of life, like a beacon lighting the path of the child, the adolescent and the young person".[23]

The Catechist

9. The simplest guideline for the parent or catechist of children should be never to teach anything that needs to be "untaught" later and always to respect the human and christian dignity of even the tiniest child. The catechist, whether of the "domestic church", school or parish, should remember his vital role[24] and while being heartened by his privilege of sharing in the apostolic work[25] at the same time should recognise his need for constant growth in his own understanding of the faith. All the documents cited above have in common this expression of the constant need on the part of the catechist to grow in his own faith, to take advantage of the increasing opportunities for adult christian education offered at parochial and deanery level. He needs to deepen his own understanding of Scripture that its message may activate his life and so that his participation in liturgical worship may become more fruitful. It is his own living faith he will share with the child. Because it is a child he teaches, he needs to take trouble to be aware of the situation in which he is the guide; to recognise the particular stage of spiritual and intellectual development reached by the learner and so to apply appropriate methods for success in each particular case. For this he needs to become more conscious of the way in which a child's understanding grows and develops, taking advantage of the insights gained over recent years, particularly by child psychologists and experts in education. But first he needs to look at childhood itself to see why it is that this state, in its own right, is so important in the process of human maturing and therefore for spiritual development.

Childhood

10. This whole period, from the age of about four to eleven or twelve, has special significance in the making of a Christian. The child is being prepared for life as a fully mature christian adult: "one who has made a free and reflective commitment to Christ in his Church".[26] It is of vital importance, however, to remember that each day and from day to day this same child is living his christian life NOW and should be helped to do so as fully and maturely as his present stage of human development allows. He is not a miniature adult, he is not only in a stage of "preparing to be", he IS now. Already he has an existing relationship with the Trinity which it is the catechist's privilege and duty to foster.

11. This essential importance of childhood for its own sake, as well as a stage of total growth, was developed by Karl Rahner in a lecture on *Ideas for a Theology of Childhood.* After speaking of "the direct relationship with God which is achieved at each of the stages of human development" he identifies "the unique and unrepeatable value attached to childhood in particular". He points out that it is during childhood that the foundations are laid for future decisions which will affect not only the kind of person he is and the kind of career he will embark upon, but "which will have an eternal significance". He then describes the importance of childhood as the "point of departure for the adult man" since it influences the future choices open to him and, because of this, on what will "finally take place when the individual's life comes to its close". Most people would agree with all this. Indeed, it is at the base of most of the arguments about vocational or academic education, about the kinds of schools and places of further education which should be available and the curriculum they should offer.

Rahner, however, suggests next that "more than this it is important in itself also, as a stage of man's personal history in which that takes place which can only take place in childhood itself, a field which bears fair flowers and ripe fruits such as can only grow in this field and in no other, and which will themselves be carried into the storehouses of eternity". Those who have watched the absorption of children at work or at play, or noted their spontaneous generosity, who have prayed with them, or who have celebrated with them, sharing their joy in a well-prepared liturgy, can only endorse this. Later on, Rahner repeats: "The grace of childhood is not merely the pledge of the grace of adulthood" insisting further that "it must be the case that childhood is valuable in itself, for it is to be discovered anew in the ineffable future which is coming to meet us". It is in this way that Rahner interprets Matthew 18:3-4 and underlines all he has said by the simple statement that Christianity "has reverence for the child, for the child is a man".

Catechesis in Childhood

12. We must all recognise, therefore, that the cetechesis of chilhood is important because it prepares for "a free response to the grace of the revealing God"[27] when full adult maturity is reached. Of even greater importance is the catechesis of childhood to the child himself now, at the present moment, since each year is non-repeatable and at each stage the child is living a particular relationship with God which "flowers" in eternity. This is why all who teach, whether professionally or otherwise need to understand how, in fact, a child's faith develops: what can profitably be taught or undertaken at the different stages and what may simply cause confusion or even build up towards disaster. It is important always for catechists to keep in mind, that faith is not to be measured by intellectual understanding, nor is the quality of a child's faith to be gauged by his ability to define what he believes. It is worthy of note in this connection that outstanding work continues to be done in catechesis for the mentally handicapped. Here it is the love, patience and skill of the small community of believers, in sharing their own faith, which stimulates the faith response in the handicapped child. It is wisely said that religion is caught, not taught.

Only general points will be made here because it will be more useful to work out precise implications later as we consider the child's introduction to Scripture and initiation into prayer and sacramental understanding.

Infancy

13. Before the child grows from infancy into childhood he is at the stage which, in other contexts, is termed pre-catechesis. That is, his ordinary human relationships will be preparing the ground for the catechesis to come. It is because he is loved unconditionally by his parents that he can later really believe that, despite his unworthiness, God loves him. He first learns trust from his mother who responds to all his needs of body and mind; from his father's strength and ability to "put things right". Normally it is as a result of such experience that he can learn faith and trust in God. To speak to God and "share" in worship can only be by imitation and because it pleases those he has learned to love.

A child whose early experience is less fortunate will need even more the care and support of a loving christian community. Most catechists, priests and teachers can bear witness to the powerful action of the Holy Spirit in the lives of individual children whose first environment would seem to destroy any hope that the baptismal faith would come to fruition. In his exhortation *Catechesis in Our Time,* Pope John Paul II speaks of "an ever increasing number of children and young people born and brought up in a non-christian or at least non-practising home but who wish to know the christian faith. They must be ensured a catechesis attuned to them, so that they will be able to grow in faith and live by it more and more, in spite of the lack of support or even the opposition they meet in their surroundings".[28]

Early Childhood

14. As the infant passes into early childhood true catechesis can begin, most happily if, as previously indicated, the adult world surrounding him is at one in faith. Otherwise there is the risk that his "religious world" will become merely a part of his fantasy world, which is a feature of this stage of growth between the ages of about four and seven, for he is not always able to distinguish between the real world and his own inner world of fantasy which he will leave behind, as he explores and grasps the real world in middle and later childhood. He now enters a period of steady growth and emotional stability, for the tantrums of infancy are past and the storms of adolescence, if any, are still to come.

15. During these years which, in this country, correspond with starting school and becoming established as an "Infant", he is still the centre of his own world and cannot see things from another person's point of view. He is dependent upon his own perception of reality. If his family experience has so far been good, he is ready to learn to know God our Father, who loves him and surrounds him with proofs of his love in the people who care for him and the beauty he enjoys. He can be helped to respond to this love. Above all, one should avoid presenting a vindictive God who is just watching out to see when he is "naughty". The young child has a great capacity for wonder and perhaps the adult will need to regain his own sense of wonder if he is to help him in the first steps of prayer. True reasoning is beyond him since he can see only one relationship at a time so it is useless to expect him to follow a process of logical thought, or to be able to draw conclusions. Doctrinal statements, which he can easily repeat to please, will hold no meaning for him. He can recognise the goodness of God our Father in sending Jesus to show us his love, but it is a strong, grown-up Jesus we want him to get to know for, at this age, a child's "best friends" are adults whom he trusts and upon whom he relies. When he is told of Jesus choosing special friends, he can begin to understand that he, too, is a friend of Jesus. This young child lives in the here and now; time past has little meaning, nor have far away places. It is vital, therefore, that he meets the living Christ of today and does not think of him always as one who lived a long time ago in a distant land.

16. One needs to be most careful, towards the end of this period, as the child begins to be introduced to sacramental life for there is a risk that the magical attitudes of his fairy-tale world may be transferred into his attitude to sacraments. In his world, animals talk, while tables and chairs, which he does not recognise as inanimate, may bang against him and hurt him. With poor teaching, sacraments may become part of this magic and the idea, once established, becomes difficult to eradicate. Sacramental teaching for Juniors will be centred upon the recognition that sacraments are meetings with Christ in faith. They presuppose faith, express faith and increase faith. Sacramental preparation will be concerned more with fostering the faith response in the child than with correct performance of external ritual words and acts. For the same reason, it is unwise to dwell upon the miraculous in the life of Jesus, lest he should become for the child little more than a magician. Stories of Jesus healing the sick, the blind and the lame will be told to show his creative love meeting the needs of all who turn to him in trust, restoring wholeness, whether the disease be physical or spiritual.

For the child at this stage, stories are one of the great joys of his life. Since his power over language is increasing, he loves to talk with an adult about his stories which can provide plenty of opportunity for early exploration of relationships and initiation into ideas of right and wrong, if the adult seizes the opportunities provided, without moralising. Always we need to remember that it is Good News that we are telling, so the imparting of it should bring only joy and happiness.

Middle and Later Childhood

17. During middle and later childhood (roughly seven to nine and ten to twelve) the child is passing through what psychologists call the concrete operational stage, that is, although he is not yet capable of truly abstract reasoning, he can reason when working with real objects and draw conclusions from his own real experiences, or vicarious experiences presented to him by story or by other concrete media; hence the need for a child to be helped to think about his own human experience and to participate in religious experience. It is only towards the very end of this "Junior" stage that most children begin to be able to think abstractly, so throughout childhood it is still too early to expect formal religious language to be understood. It should be noted, though, that Juniors learn by heart very easily and love repeating formulae and rigmarole (listen to them at play!), but adults should not be taken in by their fluency: it could be mere verbalism. Yet it would be foolish to miss taking advantage of this stage when a store of worthwhile and previously understood religious ideas can be so easily memorised.

The child's social sense and sense of responsibility develops throughout this period. His "gang" loyalties can be channelled into real christian concern for those less fortunate than himself. Because he is becoming more aware of personal relationships with those around him, it is during this time that a real devotion to the person of Christ can be fostered, to be expressed in loyalty and loving service. The passion and death of Christ will be shown as the supreme act of love. Otherwise, there is a danger here, again, of presenting the Father as a vindictive tyrant who demanded torment and suffering from his Son.

18. The Junior loves to write, to draw, to act, to sing, to join with his group in creating models and works of art of many kinds. All this activity can be used to advantage in helping him to think more deeply about the experiences he is recording. He finds it difficult to sit still and meditate, but his activity can, with guidance, in very truth be meditative prayer. The finished products of his imagination, crude though they might be from the artistic point of view, will remain for some time to stimulate his thinking and deepen the effect. This is particularly true if a sensitive adult questions and discusses while he is working and after the product is complete. From this, also, he can be led to understand that it is one's work, the product of mind, senses and will, the total self, that is offered to God through Christ in the Eucharist.

Creativity can lead on into a deeper appreciation of the wonder that is man. Before he reaches the uncertainties of adolescence, he should be helped to recognise his own unique value in the eyes of God. It is in this same context that he can be given more formal sex education. The Junior is avid for the latest knowledge. He admires technology and can be led on to wonder at man's inventive power; to recognise his consequent responsibility. Thus it becomes possible for his teacher to make relevant the message of Genesis 2:15 where man is placed in charge of God's creation "to till the earth and take care of it". In this same context, basic positive teaching can be given on the nature and source of human rights and the insult offered to God in their denial.

Christ: The Focus for Catechesis

19. Throughout the years of childhood, as indeed on through adulthood, Christ will be the centre and focal point of all catechesis. In the first encyclical of his pontificate John Paul II reminds us forcefully: "In Christ and through Christ God has revealed himself fully to mankind and has definitively drawn close to it; at the same time, in Christ and through Christ man has acquired full awareness of his dignity, of the heights to which he is raised, of the surpassing worth of his own humanity, and of the meaning of his existence",[29] and so the catechesis will ensure that the Scriptures will be shown to be totally about Christ. The Old Testament tells of the preparation of man for the coming of Christ and the New the meaning of the presence of Christ in the world of man. The sacraments will be presented as meetings with Christ, giving and restoring life, healing, nourishing, strengthening and empowering. Morality will become a response to Christ who shows us the Father.[30] If we follow his way, he leads us to the Father. He not only shows us the way, he IS "the Way, the Truth, and the Life".[31] The catechist of children sets their feet upon this path, walking the way by their side.

FURTHER REFERENCES:

The Rite of Baptism for Children, commentary E. Yarnold, St Paul Publications;

Ideas for a Theology of Childhood, K. Rahner, Lecture at Second International Convention S.O.S. Children's Villages;

G.C.D. 17-21; 31; 35; 37-40; 45-46; 71-75; 78-81; 113-115;

T.F.N.W. p. 1-5; p. 8-9; 30-31; 134-136; 148-152; 154-157; 185-189; 195-196;

The Redeemer of Mankind (Redemptor Hominis), Pope John Paul II, CTS;

C.T. 20-25; 31; 35-45; 67-69.

USEFUL FOR PARENTS AND TEACHERS:

Together at Baptism, Payne, Ave Maria Press;
Parents, Children and God, Bullen, Fontana.

NOTES:

[1] GCD 20
[2] Cf. 1 Pet 3:15
[3] TFNW 124
[4] ALP 11
[5] DCE 8
[6] Cornerstone 49; 50
[7] Rite of Baptism for Children, p. 38
[8] CS 73
[9] Ibid 49
[10] Ibid 50
[11] Rite, p. 33
[12] GCD 107
[13] TFNW 31
[14] GCD 2-9
[15] Rom 8:9
[16] Rom 8:21
[17] TFNW 92
[18] CT 56
[19] Ibid 35
[20] Ibid 36
[21] Ibid 37
[22] Cornerstone 17
[23] CT 39
[24] DCMA 17
[25] Cf. 1 Thess 2:2-8
[26] Cornerstone 50
[27] GCD 3
[28] CT 42
[29] Redemptor Hominis 11
[30] Jn 14:8-11
[31] Jn 14:6

PART TWO

2.

Catechesis through Experience and Themes

(cf. Cornerstone: 171-186)

Reasons for these Methods

20. Many teachers and, perhaps even more parents, especially those whose own religious education was firmly based upon the catechism, tend to suspect methods of teaching religion which make great use of human experience. They consider, perhaps, that a good deal of time is wasted on "experiences" and "themes" which might be better spent upon the direct transmission of religious ideas. Sometimes they may be right, but in judging these approaches it is necessary first to understand the thought behind them, especially when they are used with children of the junior age-group.

They are not a "gimmick", nor a way chosen by the uncommitted of avoiding teaching "real religion". In practice, they make greater demands upon the teacher's theological understanding and powers of organisation. The basis is an incarnational whole-life approach, to help the child to see ordinary, daily life from God's viewpoint; to help him to see that God speaks to us day by day through ordinary happenings. There is no denying that this way is in keeping with the manner in which the junior child thinks and acts, with his holistic approach to life. It is, most importantly, the way of teaching of Christ himself, who drew from the ordinary experiences of the daily lives of his listeners, in order to lead them to his Father. The child, at home and in school, is living his christian life NOW, and needs help to interpret and develop his daily experience, to see that Christianity is for living, not just for learning, that ALL his living is to be made christian, not just religion lessons and part of Sunday morning.

Choosing and Planning

21. An approach is purposeless unless it leads somewhere and a guide is useless unless he knows his present position and the best way to reach his destination. Therefore, the teacher must be clearly aware of two things; the present situation of the child and the religious idea he wishes the child to understand and appreciate. Then he needs to structure his material, in accordance with the child's ability and interests, so that learning can take place — otherwise, we risk the trivialisation of religious truth. The choice of a theme topic demands both perception and sensitivity on the part of the teacher, since it must be evidently and immediately relevant to the child's present educational stage. For the junior, there must be just one basic idea which, in itself, is worth exploring in depth. Themes suggested in a good syllabus will normally meet these demands, but the teacher needs to read and interpret the mind of the planner, or he will be lost in a morass of detail and the logical sequence will be dimmed.

Aims and Objectives

22. The *Directory on Children's Masses* urges that those "who are concerned with education should work and plan together to ensure that children, besides having some idea of God and the supernatural, should also, in proportion to their years and maturity as persons, have some experience of those human values which are involved in Eucharistic celebration".[1] So the teacher will ascertain and define his precise aim: the aspect of religious truth to be taught and the attitudes to be fostered. Then he will determine the human values which it is possible to explore, starting from the child's present experience. Before the planning is complete, specific objectives will have been set for each stage or session of teaching.

The Basic Process

23. The process of teaching a religious theme will be unique

to the individual teacher and the actual group being taught, but there are some general guidelines which can be followed. Some time will be spent on considering the basic experience. There may only be the need to identify and recall a common experience. Sometimes it will be necessary to supply or even to correct, where there is known to be inadequate or unfortunate previous experience. Always there is the need to build upon and widen, to encourage deeper appreciation. The content will be approached from as many different angles as possible, using all relevant school disciplines. As the opportunity arises, an incident from Scripture will be used to enlighten and so also to demonstrate the perennial relevance of God's word. All the time the child will be led to discover in how many ways the new perceptions can flow out into personal prayer or paraliturgy and directly into his way of life at home, in school, in his peer group or, in the case of the older child, into wider social settings. Where practicable, some appropriate action will be considered, planned and executed. Finally, as a group, adult and children together will celebrate this new stage of spiritual development in liturgy or paraliturgy. " . . . Active pedagogy should not be satisfied with external expressions only, however useful they may be, but should strive to bring forth a response from the heart and a taste for prayer".[2]

FURTHER REFERENCE:

G.C.D. 26; 46; 74.
T.F.N.W. 118-21; 179;
C.T. 22.

NOTES:

[1] DCM 9
[2] GCD 79

3.

The Message of Scripture

(cf. Cornerstone 122; 127-39)

Why teach Scripture to Children?

24. We must accept, first of all, that there can be no over-simple approach to teaching Scripture to children; the Bible is an adult book — written by adults for adults — and never intended as a "story-book" for children. There are many stumbling-blocks and difficulties. Yet it is "the word of God in the words of men"; it contains the deeds and intentions of God. All true christian teaching is based on Scripture. Indeed, right up to the thirteenth century all theology was a commentary on Scripture. Therefore, as teachers or as parents, we have no choice: it is our duty to present the Scriptures to children, but to present in such a way that they truly become "good tidings of great joy" and not the comings and goings of middle-eastern tribes around two thousand years ago.

God is Revealed

25. So Scripture needs to be taught in a way appropriate to children. We need to help their growing intellects to recognise something of the wonder of revelation unfolded in Scripture. We need to foster attitudes which will enable them to respond to God's revelation of himself — Father, Son and Spirit. *We* must realise, if we are to help *them* to realise, that God is revealing himself to them now — that they must be open to this revelation, so that they can respond. We will use Scripture with children to "hold up a mirror to life" so that the experience of over two thousand years of man's relationship with God, contained in Scripture, will light up their present experience.[1]

Getting to know God

26. Learning Scripture should be an on-going process of "getting to know you". Just as we recognise an author, a musician, an artist, by his style so we get to know God by his deeds. "At various times in the past and in various different ways, God spoke to our ancestors through the prophets; but in our own time, the last days, he has spoken to us through his Son".[2] The Scriptures tell what we know for certain about God — his own self-revelation. How, then, should it be taught? As God himself does: he told a story: he put himself in the story — the story of all sorts of people, who, like ourselves, are good, bad or indifferent. God is the hero of the story — not Abraham, Moses, David. It is the story of how people like us reacted to him. It is the story of what God said and did.

The Process

27. Basically the manner of using Scripture is the same with any age-group. The process is the same, the method will be different. We take an incident — a story, a piece of teaching, a parable — and see it in context. This is important because it will affect the way we tell the story to young children or the way we present the text for the older child to study. Sometimes it is easy to place a passage in context. The Good Samaritan would not present many difficulties to most of us; but sometimes it can be very difficult; what is the context of Genesis 1-11? Once it is in context, it is possible to establish what is happening, i.e., what it is that the divine and human author wish to convey. The Bible is for all times, for all peoples, so it has a message for us, today.[3] We need to be receptive, to help the children to be receptive; so it is not enough to stop at "what happened"; we need to discover the religious message. This sometimes means seeing the Old Testament in the light of the New — seeing our own baptism foreshadowed in the Covenant with Moses. Most of all, it means finding the personal relevance to those we teach. This does not imply moralising, rather leading them through dialogue to see "that is the sort of person God is; that is the person to whom we pray". The rule of the teacher is not to teach the Bible (as one would teach a play of Shakespeare) but to help the children to discover religious truth. Therefore, the aim is not to encourage the children to ask: did it really happen? is it really true? but rather to ask: what does it mean?

The Purpose

28. Children up to the age of twelve or thirteen — perhaps even later are not yet capable of a synthetic view of time, so we cannot teach them the story of salvation as such, rather we need to show them "the wonderful works of God" in the Old Testament, and to show them how the discourses, events, miracles of the New Testament lead us to an understanding of Christ today, as he acts in us, in his Church, in his mystical body.

In Early Childhood

29. With very small children, it is a case of getting to know the God about whom the adults talk and to whom they pray. We tell the stories, little more than the stories, so that each makes its own impact. Avoid giving too much, too soon; not all are suitable for the first years of childhood, so careful choice must be made. This is one of the advantages of following a good syllabus in the infant school, where stories are suggested with clear relevance to the child's daily experience. Young children "live" their stories if they are told vividly, immediately, giving them the opportunity to identify, to mingle with the crowd, to watch what goes on, what is said, thought, to watch the reactions. In this way, they come to know how God's friends acted, what Jesus did, how he talked and acted with his friends, and how they responded, how he met the needs of those around him. We encourage the children's response, sometimes supplying words to help them to formulate prayer. In this way, we foster the relationship, entered at baptism, between the child and God, Father, Son and Spirit.

Jesus' own Method: How and Why

30. A teacher, or a parent teaching a growing child, can gladly recognise in Jesus' own teaching methods approaches ideally suited to the junior at the concrete stage of learning. Jesus conveyed the mysteries of the kingdom to ordinary men — fisher-folk, farmers, housewives, small tradesmen. As they listened, the abstract became concrete: they learned of God's care for each one of us as they observed the lilies of the field, the birds of the air. For them, as for us, even the youngest of us, the invisible becomes visible as he talks of water, of bread and wine, of sowing and reaping, of building, of mending clothes, of losing and finding, of baking, of journeys and homecomings. So, in our own teaching there should be no premature use of technical words, no excess of systematisation. Still, at this stage, there is risk of giving too much too soon, of choosing inappropriate material. The parable of the prodigal son, told as a "nice story" to the eight-year-old, can then become stale and perhaps even useless for the teenager preparing for the sacrament of reconciliation. Each time we need to pose to ourselves the question: how will this particular passage nourish these children's faith and piety? The stories of Abraham, Moses, David are not biographies and, indeed, it is a waste of time to tell their stories if we do not get over the religious meaning, if we do not help the children to ponder their converse with God. We tell their stories to show the import of their lives and acts.

Finding and Giving the Message

31. Often, in Scripture, the message is complex; often, in one incident there are several "messages". The younger the child, the more necessary it becomes to concentrate upon one and so to narrate the event that this is brought out. The rest can be left for someone else, in another context. Here again we see the value of a good syllabus where the incident will be chosen because it illumines some special aspect of the theme being taught, a theme appropriate to the child's present stage of experience and development. In any case, the passage should be chosen because it throws light upon some idea, some relationship, which it is right and possible for the child to explore now.

Obtaining a Response: The Barriers

32. We need to bring children to see that the people in the Bible are not weird inhabitants of another magical world but people like us and the people around us. What was Adam's first thought on being found out? Blame someone else! Jacob did not find telling lies too high a price to pay for an inheritance. David found it easy to fight gloriously in God's battles, not so easy to obey his commandments. He could dance for joy, he could also fall miserably into sin. Peter, full of courage for a time, could later the same day deny his master. The priest on the road to Jericho — was he a bad man? Perhaps he just did not want to get involved. All this, of course, underlines the fact that with children we cannot just tell the story straight and hope to let it make its own impact. Even less can we hope that by reading the story for themselves without guidance, much will be gained. Scripture demands a response of the heart. A response cannot be forced, but it can be prevented; the story must be so told that a response can be obtained. Nearly always with children, there are two sorts of barriers to be overcome; the knowledge barrier and the experience barrier. We must ensure that there is sufficient background knowledge so that the message gets through. This may involve something as simple as explaining a word or it may mean some time spent on exploring the human or historical background. The experience barrier is not such a problem if the passage chosen is appropriate to the child's stage of development. We need to ascertain whether these particular children have been in a similar situation. If so, will they recognise it, or will perhaps a few words recall and enliven it? If not, perhaps because their background is impoverished or restricted, can we supply an experience either directly or vicariously which will enable the child to appreciate the scriptural situation?

Middle and Later Childhood

33. During the years of later childhood the story remains the chief means of mediating the message of Scripture. Indeed, the re-emphasis on the liturgy of the word in sacramental rites has demonstrated that this is a life-long need. As they grow, we help children to recognise the "treasures old and new" that Scripture can reveal for every age and situation. Parent, catechist, teacher, priest, all need to reflect on the deeper and different messages for this particular child or group at this specific stage. Opportunities are constantly presented: it could be a child's question, or an event occurring at home; it could be a particular moment of enlightenment during the exploration of a theme; it could be while penetrating the symbolism of a sacrament: each could provide the moment when the message is given with greater effect.

Gradually now we widen and deepen the children's scriptural experience. The Bible itself is introduced as the source of all the stories. A well-printed, well-illustrated copy, used with reverence and respect by the adult, will be an attraction and a delight to the child. The story will be woven into a theme being explored to develop understanding and appreciation of a human relationship or situation. Juniors are avid collectors, so this is the time to supply information about the background of biblical life and times. These children love using information books, filmstrips, picture atlases to make their own books and models. They gradually accumulate knowledge which helps them later to appreciate that the Bible "characters" were real people, that "spiritually we are all semites" and that Christ is truly man — who walked on dusty roads, ate home-baked bread, wore the same sort of clothes as every other man of his home village, in days when his country was occupied by a foreign power.

Teaching the Bible "Story"

34. Before children enter the stage of teenage doubt and cynicism through which many pass, there is need to begin another process which, for most of us, is also life-long. They need to take their first straight look at the Bible itself: what it is and what it is not; how it came first to be transmitted, orally, sometimes as camp-fire stories, and later to be written down by many human authors, each with his own style and with the knowledge of a man of his age; written down over a period of about a thousand years; that the Bible is not one, but many books; that all these books are true; that truth can be expressed in many forms — scientific, poetical, historical — but that in Scripture it is theological truth that we are seeking and that this can be expressed in many literary forms; that not all these books are of equal value; that ALL these books are about God's initiative and man's response. It is, of course, essential to note that we do not "teach" all this as "lessons". This is the beginning of a process which will continue at least throughout the secondary stage of education. At first we arouse interest, rather than exhaust possibilities; we deal only with what is within their own experience, or soon will be; we do not seek to impose adult ideas.

Methods with Older Children

35. In later childhood and early adolescence more sophisticated methods of studying a Scripture passage can be used. After introductory work in class, or discussion with an adult, a work-card can help the child to interiorise what has been learned. A well-planned card will lead from the establishing of fact to the consideration of motive and then, more importantly, to the application of the scriptural ideas to the child's own personal life or understanding of liturgy. Guided group discussions or Bible probes, short and on quite specific points, will prepare children for the later process of "see, judge, act" used, for example, in YCW work. Always we start from their own experience, with their own needs in mind, although this does necessarily mean that we start *with* their own experience. Quite simple theme studies will deepen liturgical appreciation. For example, an exploration of what Jesus did at meals will help eucharistic understanding. This also prepares the way for a later study of biblical themes.

So from later childhood onwards both processes continue: discovering the message of the Bible and understanding the Bible itself. More and more the processes become interwoven as the exploration goes on: what kind of people the prophets were; why the epistles were written; what was Jesus' attitude towards women, the poor, political authority. All this, of course, occurs at a much later stage than childhood.

FURTHER REFERENCES:

GCD	10-16; 32;
TFNW	102-108; 164-165;
CT	6-11; 26-27:

USEFUL FOR PARENTS AND TEACHERS:

Listen!, McCallen (Collins);

Praise!, McCallen (Collins);

The King's Donkey Series, Richardson (Mayhew McCrimmon);

The Rainbow Series (CIO).

NOTES:

[1] Cf. DCDR 7
[2] Heb 1:1-2
[3] 2 Pet 1:20

4.

Helping Children to Pray

(cf. Cornerstone: 51a; 53-56)

The priority of Prayer

36. "If a child has learned to pray, we have achieved everything; if he doesn't know how to pray, we have failed". This injunction offered to teachers by the pioneer catechist Fr Tilmann, should set our priorities both at home and in school. Prayer is learned, is "caught", by a kind of osmosis, by absorbing the attitudes of parents, in the first case, and later those of teachers and other adults. The good home, where prayer is practised, is the best place for a child to learn to pray. Liturgical prayer is "soaked in" by the child in his parish church, where the liturgy is celebrated effectively, vitally, joyfully. The work of the school, therefore, is to sustain, to foster, to extend understanding, to provide opportunities for communal worship of this particular christian unit or group within it and, unfortunately, where others fail, to try to supply the lack.

Response: Speaking and Listening

37. Prayer is man's response in faith to the living God. Our over-all aim is to help the children to see that our first and greatest answer to God all our life — as child, as adult — is our life as it is lived, that our way of speaking with God must grow spontaneously from our way of life; that because of his baptism "a Christian's life can never be profane . . . but is wholly a life of worship".[1] The first quality of prayer is surely recognition of the greatness and wonder of God, his love for us and our utter dependence upon him for all we have and are, for everything

in the order of nature and of grace. The youngest infant in school will tell us that prayer is "talking to God". This is good; the idea is scriptural: Adam, Abraham, Moses, Samuel, Isaiah "talked with God". We need probably to point out that also they all listened — and acted upon what they had heard. We want the children to recognise that prayer is not an occasional duty, still less a mechanical gesture, but a loving response to a superabundant love.

How Prayer is Learned

38. The task, then, of the adult helping the child to pray is fourfold: to help him to pray spontaneously, in simple, direct words; to teach some of the formal prayers of the Church, so that he can PRAY them; to help him towards mental prayer; to encourage him to pray liturgically, helping him to begin to understand that all prayer is an entering in to the prayer of Christ, the redemptive act of Christ. With older children there may be lessons or discussions on the nature of prayer itself but, if so, these will be few and occasional. Mostly teaching will be incidental, occasioned by the place prayer has in the home and the school. Do we, in fact, pray together? Is it important enough to have time set aside for it? Do we encourage recollection, relaxed and reverent posture, moments of silence? After prayers of petition, do we suggest thanks? How do we deal with the "naughty" child who is distracting others? Not, it is hoped, by a total destruction of the atmosphere of prayer.

Gesture and Movement; Music

39. A child can often express prayer in gesture and in mime, sometimes when he is quite incapable of giving expression to his thoughts in word. This can and should be encouraged and helped by a sensitive adult, but, just as expression in word can become mere verbalism if it is forced beyond understanding, so gesture and mime could deteriorate into formalism — almost into puppetry — where the external act becomes insincere. The response is then to the suggestion of the adult and not to interior prompting.

With most children and especially with young children, music can be an invaluable aid to prayer. It is best if the melody is attractive, memorable and attuned to the child's stage of development. There is an old saying that he who sings hymns prays twice. This takes for granted that the words will be appropriate to both his intellectual and spiritual growth, so that he can mean and pray them.[2] "A hymn that is sung by all the children in common denotes a high degree of self-activity on their part. Because of its musical and practical sound structure, and because it represents an achievement of their own, it is something which the children greatly enjoy".[3]

Formal Teaching

40. Frequently, though by no means always, prayer will be an integral part of a religion lesson, where thinking around a scripture story or discussing some relationship or situation will lead naturally to a simple, spontaneous formulation in the teacher's own words, to the "turning" and personalising of the biblical words, to the expressing of the thought in a well-known prayer, section of a prayer, or verse of a psalm, or to making a "collect" from the children's ideas. It is wise to remember that children, like all of us, cannot pray to order and that if the request to "make up a prayer" is presented insensitively and without suitable stimulus, it can encourage the building up of a "penny-in-the-slot" response which is mere verbalism and therefore counter-productive. When the subject lends itself, simple litanies, perhaps in the style of bidding prayers, will allow the adults to guide children's thinking and yet retain their active involvement. Sometimes it is necessary, particularly in later childhood, to "rescue" a familiar prayer, such as the Our Father or the Hail Mary — or any prayer in frequent use, perhaps during family prayer or at the school assembly — by ensuring that the words have not disintegrated into meaningless jargon and by searching into the meaning of the phrases in a way appropriate to the child's present age, so that the prayer grows in depth of meaning as the child grows. The adult will need to be ready to deal with the problems children raise: the seemingly unanswered prayer; does not God know what we want already? Are we asking God to change his mind?

Liturgical Prayer

41. At home and in school, liturgical prayer is best taught, as we follow through the Church's year, helping the children year by year to personalise the mysteries. Here again, a good syllabus can be invaluable, particularly if parents and teachers are working in conjunction, for at each stage a different aspect of the mystery will be explored and each year a greater depth of understanding and appreciation becomes possible, while repetition, leading only to boredom is avoided. The same applies in preparation for sacramental celebration. Life-themes explore, year by year, different aspects of sacramental symbolism. In school, but also at home, a paraliturgical celebration as the culmination of several sessions of work, can provide children with the opportunity to interiorise each stage of development in understanding. So we shall help them to pray the Mass, rather than to pray at Mass, in a manner suitable to their stage of spiritual growth. We can help them to understand the prayers of the Mass, not only by explaining, but also by using them, or part of them, in an appropriate way in daily prayer. Using Collects, perhaps in simplified form, can give early insight into praying in true liturgical form, at the same time helping to avoid childish confusion in the persons of the Trinity. The child learns to pray to God, our Father, who loves and provides for us; through the Son, Jesus our Brother, who redeems us and brings us to his Father; in the power of the Holy Spirit who helps us and dwells within us. The Curé of Ars once said: "The best way of conversing with God is to speak to him as if he were a man. Christ has made this possible for us". That is why God the Son became man, that man might be enabled to make the perfect response to God. Education in liturgical prayer enables the child to begin to understand the phrase "through Jesus Christ our Lord" and to mean it when he says it; enables him to see that every prayer we pray unites us to the mystery we celebrate at Mass.

Feasts and Devotions

42. The priority of liturgical prayer does not mean that we ignore devotion to our Lady and the saints. Fr Hofinger frequently warned teachers that what he called a "proliferation of devotions" could come between children and true worship. Parents and other adults could also keep this in mind and ensure as they celebrate the feastdays with children, that all is done within the perspective of christian worship. The feasts of our Lady, the mysteries of the Rosary, each express a particular relationship with Christ who is Mary's Son. Saints' days celebrate those heroic members of the mystical body of Christ throughout the ages who lived fully the Christ-life in the circumstances of their time and environment. These men and women of every race, colour, nation, class, and condition have one thing in common: in whatever historical setting they were placed each, in his own way, portrayed Christ to his neighbour; made to the Father the christian response. If we examine the Collects of the propers of saints we find these two aspects are always clearly expressed. After children have been involved in the story of some incident in the saint's life, they can be led by dialogue to formulate a prayer which, like the formal collect, will help them to identify the reason why the Church, by canonisation, offers this saint for our admiration and emulation.

Private Prayer and Public Worship

43. The *General Catechetical Directory* summarises the catechetical function of the adult in the christian community when it stipulates that: "catechesis must promote an active, conscious, genuine participation in the liturgy of the Church . . . The Christian is assuredly called to pray with his brethren, but he must also enter into his chamber to pray to the Father in secret . . . Therefore, catechesis must also train the faithful to meditate on the word of God and to engage in private prayer".[4]

FURTHER REFERENCES:

GCD	25;
TFNW	135, 136, 152;
CT	36, 47, 54.

USEFUL FOR PARENTS AND TEACHERS:

Teach Us to Pray, St Paul Publications

NOTES:

[1] Durwell, *In the Redeeming Christ,* p. 184
[2] DCM 30-32
[3] Jungmann, *Handing on the Faith,* p. 268
[4] GCD 25

5.

Fostering a Sacramental Understanding

(cf. Cornerstone 51a; 155-170; 200-209; 214; 218)

God Communicates Through the Senses

44. Catechesis during childhood is mainly concerned with preparation for present and future sacramental meetings with Christ; with learning to appreciate that: "I AM baptised"; that this is not an event of the past but that the whole of life and the way it is lived is a response, a verification of the "putting on" of Christ at Baptism. The child gradually learns that, since man can only acquire knowledge through the senses, can only communicate through his senses, God communicates with man through ordinary means. Christ chose material, sensible things to be the means whereby he would communicate his life to us. That which is perceptible to the senses, shows us the nature of his communication. Christ gives life, nourishes this life, strengthens and, when necessary, restores the life. The material things which Christ chose show us how he is acting. The Church surrounds each sacramental act with a rite which enhances, deepens, clarifies the meaning (as a gem is displayed by its setting).

Liturgy Teaches

45. That is why, through the ages, sacramental liturgy has been one of the most obvious means of catechesis. The liturgical signs and symbols are there for all to read, but we must learn how to read them, if we are to understand their meaning. What is obvious in one age or culture can have less significance in another time or environment. What is natural in an agricultural setting may seem incomprehensible in an inner-city area. Hence as time passes, rite and liturgy will change, if it is not to obstruct meaning. So the *Constitution on the Sacred Liturgy* ordained that the sacramental rites should be revised to clarify the symbolism and to encourage active participation.[1] The rites are now revised, but can still need interpretation, even for the adult and even despite the extension in each case of the liturgy of the word. How much the more so, then, is such interpretation necessary in the case of a child. The teacher's main task becomes one of mediation.

Teaching Symbolism

46. During childhood sacramental catechesis will be a gradual unfolding of the meaning of the rite, the sign, the symbol to deepen and extend understanding of the symbolism. One might even say that, in these years, sacramental teaching consists of exploring the symbolism ever more deeply. For early childhood there will be pre-catechesis to foster the human values which enable later appreciation and response.[2] During middle and later childhood the catechist will consider the changing interests, maturing knowledge, attitudes and modes of thought in order to choose the appropriate moment to explore a particular sacramental symbol. The general method of approach will be the same in each case: first we explore the natural symbolism of the sign; this we deepen with biblical symbolism and, with background so enriched, examine the sign in its liturgical setting. Finally, all becomes truly effective for a child by celebrating the new understanding, as he shares in an actual liturgical ceremony in his parish or, if this is inopportune, in a para-liturgy at home or in school. During childhood we do not teach about sacraments: we teach some appropriate aspect of each sacrament as the child experiences its meaning in his life. In this way, truth is gradually unfolded; the child learns that always there are greater depths in the mystery to discover. It is by "knowingly and actively" participating in sacramental liturgy that we share in "the work of our redemption".[3] Such catechesis during childhood makes this increasingly possible. The purpose of this catechesis is not to explain a liturgical act nor to teach certain doctrines connected with it so that mysteries become facts. The purpose is to enable children to enter responsively into the world of symbol and celebration, not to turn it into something else.

Exploring Natural Symbolism

47. To a modern first-world child water is always there: it comes from the tap. His experience needs extending and even more he needs to think about his experience and that of children in other less-favoured environments, before he will really discover the necessity of water for life and growth, the destructive power of water. Bread can be just a sliced loaf from the shelves of the local supermarket. The town child needs to learn by experience that a slice of bread is made of many grains of wheat, that it is the work of many hands, before he will begin to fathom the meaning of the prayer at the offering of bread. When a meal is normally a canteen dinner, fish and chips collected from the local shop, or a TV snack, the child has to learn the natural symbolism of the meal which denotes unity, friendship, a sharing of life itself. Some children have learned something of the importance of oil during petrol shortage, or when the irregular visit of the oil-tanker has meant a cold home or school. They may yet need to experience the healing, strengthening, soothing and penetrating properties of oil, before its sacramental use begins to have meaning.

Scriptural Symbolism

48. These human symbols with their own intrinsic meaning, in the course of the history of God's people have gained a deeper significance. At crucial points in the history of salvation, events are recorded which add meaning. Moses led God's people from slavery to freedom through the waters of the Sea of Reeds. The people were sustained on their journey to a new life by manna. Over hundreds of years, often in conditions of captivity and exile men were chosen to hearten, to point the way, to guard against error, to rule with power — chosen and anointed with oil. The signs of the kingdom are evident as Jesus walks among men, healing body and mind, and eating "with publicans and sinners". It is over the years of childhood that all this background is gradually accumulated. A child will more fully appreciate the significance of his sacramental meetings with Christ today as he relives those meetings with the blind, the deaf, the lame, even witnesses the dead given life and the sinner brought to the joy of reconciliation. As each incident is brought vividly before him, the child recognises that there is nothing of magic here: Jesus asks for faith. Sacraments today are signs of faith which demand faith and express faith.

Liturgical Symbolism: Baptism, Confirmation

49. As the symbol becomes richer in meaning over the years of childhood, liturgy is increasingly a living experience which has deeper meaning at each particular stage. Before he reaches adolescence, the water, anointing, white garment and lighted candle of Baptism will speak to the child of the new life he has been given, of being chosen to "put on " Christ and carry the light of Christ to others. He will have begun to interpret the signs of the Spirit, the mighty wind and the fire. His knowledge of the Holy Spirit will have been increased by learning what that spirit does in the history of salvation, by witnessing the power of the Spirit of God in Scripture to create, to animate, to transform. The work of the Spirit in the Church from the beginning, evidenced particularly in the lives of the saints and in those today who are activated by his inspiration, will inspire the child, too. Later he will understand how the imposition of the bishop's hands expresses the gift of the power of the Spirit, how the anointing with oil seals the choice to be a witness to Christ.

Early Formation of Conscience

50. The formation of a child's conscience is the total product of his environment: that is, the work of all those adults, who surround him — mainly, of course, his parents — and later of his peer group. We cannot withdraw from this responsibility, because throughout, what we do — or omit to do — and what we are, will be the child's standard. Up to the age of about seven, what is right, what is wrong is dependent upon the attitude of the adult concerned. What pleases and wins praise is right; what displeases and results in blame is wrong. The extent of the wrong is measured by the extent of the disaster, or the amount of condemnation. In these early years, the formation of attitudes has priority. The most important influence is the love and security provided by parents. By observation and experience he learns to trust, to thank, to help, to be responsible, to give joy to his friends, to express regret when he has hurt and to be forgiven. Stories, games and "pretending" all reinforce. Particularly are our attitudes to justice and charity assimilated by the child and our performance in these virtues noted and emulated.

At school, he learns more from the quality of life surrounding him than from anything explicit being taught. His own relationships will partake of the quality of the inter-personal relationships expressed in day-to-day life: the attitudes of the teachers towards one another and towards the children; the relationships encouraged among the children themselves. There is need for consistency and tolerance. The child needs to be helped to understand clearly what is expected of him. The adult needs to be firm and just in handling the actual daily happenings which themselves provide teaching points. Situations can be examined on the spot; the causes of upsets, the consequences of actions; what is deliberate and what is accidental. In this way the children can be led towards a personal appreciation of the real moral values which lie beneath the external rules. If parents and teachers are humble in admitting their own mistakes and expressing sorrow, children will respond likewise and can be encouraged to renewed effort.

We all need to remember that the pre-school child and the infant-school child are still at the stage described by the American psychologist Lawrence Kohlberg[4] as the pre-moral level, his motives for action being at first fear of punishment and later hope for a reward. In the Junior school he tends to conform to what is acceptable among his peers as he passes through the next level of "conformist morality". He needs social approval, even if the "society" is that of "the gang"; it is only towards the later stages of childhood that he can be helped to acquire a respect for law and order. Kohlberg tells us that many adults do not progress morally beyond this level into the stage of autonomy where action is inspired by internalised moral principles. Experience teaches us that most adults will operate on different occasions and in different areas of morality at stages well below their normal level. Moral education in childhood, therefore, consists in helping the child to pass through the early stages of exterior morality by wise guidance, consistent treatment and by developing the ability to judge the motives which inspire action.

Response to the Person of Christ

51. During middle and later childhood, because his total catechesis is Christocentric, the child will be helped to recognise sin for what it really is, not merely the breaking of a law, but a refusal to love, a turning from God's changeless love. He will be brought to realise that repentance is a turning back to this love to be reconciled, reinstated. Our teaching aims to build a personal relationship with Christ, to show the love of Christ to which the child can make a personal response. Only on this basis can we show the Sacrament of Reconciliation itself as a meeting with the forgiving Christ in faith. At each stage of development, we examine together some incident, appropriately chosen, from which we learn just how, in fact, Jesus met the sinner. In this way, over the years, the child will have learned that meeting Jesus makes us want to do better, to make restitution;[5] Jesus has power to forgive us — and why;[6] real sorrow brings forgiveness, no matter how bad we are;[7] Jesus wants us, even if we are naughty, seeks us out and forgives us;[8] we can never be grateful enough for the sacramental meetings with Christ which help us to live his life more fully.[9]

Positive Moral Teaching

52. At the same time there is continuous positive teaching, not by moralising, but discussing some of the special thoughts which Jesus shared with his friends, sometimes in answer to their questions, often when quite large groups of people were seeking to learn about his kingdom.[10] Positive moral attitudes can be fostered by themes which consider the child's ordinary relationships at home and in school; by well-planned role-play where children act out everyday situations and in the process discover the other person's point of view — especially if, in the dialogue which follows, motives are examined. Short stories or simple moral cases can be discussed in the same way. The whole field of children's literature offers continual opportunity for the discussion of moral values. Children are able to discuss motivation and to examine cause and effect in the making and breaking of relationships, when they themselves are neither personally nor emotionally involved. From vicarious experience of this kind they learn how to handle their own situations as their social relationships extend.

Since, in later childhood, there is a natural tendency to hero-worship, Christ himself and his friends, the saints throughout the ages, will be presented in a manner to inspire admiration and emulation. It is because of their *heroic* sanctity that the Church canonises saints. Many children have an impoverished idea of saints. They may have been presented as performers of magic tricks, which children merely dismiss as being impossible to imitate, or else as "Holy Joes" and these they certainly do not want to imitate. We teach children about saints to show how they portrayed Christ to those among whom they lived, in their circumstances and in their environment. So it needs to be done in such a way that the child will be inspired to imitate. We need, of course, to demonstrate that there are people in today's world living lives of heroic virtue. It is far more effective to present children with examples of courage, of perseverance, of outstanding charity or generosity than to circumscribe them by rules and precepts which might encourage legalism, the enemy of love. In christian moral education, ideals and holiness should have the first place; rules and principles, while necessary, come second.[11]

Service of Sorrow

53. The teaching must grow with the children: they are different people at 5, at 8, at 12. Younger children need a very simple formula for Confession, but finding the words will not be a problem for a child who has shared in well thought-out Services of Sorrow appropriate to his stage of spiritual development and present needs. These will not be too frequent, perhaps once a term or in preparation for the great liturgical feasts. By the same means, the child learns to make a realistic examination of conscience.

Magical Attitude or Sacramental Mentality?

54. It is during the years of middle and later childhood, as he passes from his world of fantasy and explores the real world, that the child can acquire a truly sacramental mentality. If this growth is fostered by the catechist, any vestiges of a magical attitude to sacraments will be destroyed, instead of surviving, sometimes with disastrous results for the preservation of faith, into adolescence and possibly even into adult life.

FURTHER REFERENCE:

GCD 55-58;

TFNW 44-46; 113-116;
CT 23, 37, 48.

USEFUL FOR PARENTS AND TEACHERS:

To God with Love, BRES, St Paul Publications;
To God with Love and Sorrow, BRES, St Paul Publications;
Confirmed in Love, BRES, St Paul Publications;
At Home with God series, BRES, (many sections);
More Like Christ, McCallen, Collins;
The Forgiveness of Sins, Matthews, Collins.

NOTES:

1 CSL 21-25
2 DCM 9
3 CSL 21
4 Cf. "Moral Stages and Moralization" in *Moral Development and Behaviour* (ed.) Thomas Lickona, p. 31-53
5 Lk 19:1-10
6 Lk 5:17-26
7 Lk 6:29-32; 23:39-43
8 Lk 15:4-7
9 Lk 17:11-19
10 Mt 25:14-30; Mt 5:1-12; Mt 25:31-46; and Lk 10:25-37
11 There will be a full treatment of Moral Education and its relationship with Religious Education in another volume of "Guidelines for Religious Education".

6.

Growth in Eucharistic Understanding

(cf. Cornerstone 166-167)

The "Directory on Children's Masses"

55. It is significant that the only age-group for which the Sacred Congregation for Divine Worship has so far prepared directives is the one we are considering: "children who have not yet reached the age of pre-adolescence".[1] Declaring that "A fully christian life is unthinkable without sharing in the liturgical action which brings the faithful together to celebrate the paschal mystery",[2] the Sacred Congregation proceeds to set out directives for eucharistic catechesis and celebration with children, starting from the premise that "it must surely be spiritually harmful to them to have the experience of going to church for years without ever understanding properly what is going on".[3] Therefore, a graduated and most carefully structured catechesis will be presented during these years to enable the child to grow in both theological understanding and liturgical practice. This undoubtedly may prove one sure way to pre-empt adolescent lapsing because "the Mass is boring".

A Continuing two-fold Task

56. The catechist will be teaching eucharistic theology and liturgy at the same time as preparing the child to share fruitfully in his next Mass. So the teaching will frequently be geared to the special circumstances of the moment, including the needs of this particular child, or group of children and the particular conditions in which the celebration is to take place. It is of vital importance that as well as practical preparation for each Mass, the catechist will be deepening each time the child's understanding of what happens at Mass (Consecration), what it means (Preparation of the Gifts), what it implies (Communion and after) and what is its context (Liturgy of the Word).

What Happens at Mass

57. The whole of the Mass radiates around the Consecration, the focal point of the Eucharistic Prayer. Only if we recognise this and teach in this way can we avoid missing the wood in admiring the trees. Asked what happens here, most children and, indeed many adults will reply: "Christ is really present". This is indeed true but how inadequate to express this presence of Christ offering himself (and with us) in love to the Father; this moment in Christ's existence on earth when he gave the supreme testimony of his love for the Father and for us. We need to help the child to come to some understanding that Christ's sacrifice began from the first moment of his existence on earth; he was utterly dedicated to the loving fulfilment of his Father's will. This final free acceptance of his Father's will, the agonised forgiveness of those who crucified him, was the culmination and completion of his total life's work. It is in this supreme moment that we join when we share in the eucharistic sacrifice. The "Preparation of the Gifts" clarifies this for us, but will only do so for a child if he has been helped to see the true meaning of "gift". Why do we offer a gift to God? For the same reason as to any man. The gift represents ourselves, our attempt to express our love, thanks, sorrow when we have hurt. The giving of gifts is a natural, human thing. The gift symbolises our feelings — that is why hypocrisy destroys the essence. It is the feelings that matter, for the gift may be trivial, even useless, as are so many of the gifts children offer to their parents for Christmas or for birthdays, but the parents receive them with great joy, for it is the feeling being expressed that they value. So it is that the greatest gift is yourself, to devote yourself, to give your life, to give up your life. This is what Christ did.

Exploring "Gift" (Sacrifice)

58. To begin to appreciate this mystery the children need help, especially today when there is "a free gift in every packet" and goods are being "given away" at sales. For them, the word "gift" needs to be restored to its true meaning. The child must learn to distinguish the meaning of gift from wage, bribe, reward, before he can even begin to appreciate the meaning of giving oneself. Then, by story or experience, he will learn how a mother gives herself to a sick child, how Fr Damien gave himself to the lepers, how Mother Teresa gives herself to the dying outcasts of Calcutta. Only then will he begin to enter into the mystery of "My body which is given up for you". It was on the same night that Jesus said: "A man can have no greater love than to lay down his life for his friends".[4]

Comm-unity

59. Now, too, the Comm-union with Christ will come to have greater meaning, and so we are led back into the Liturgy of the Word, for if we are to offer our lives we must learn to live them well. Before offering, we sit down to get advice on how to offer. We have come together as God's people, needing his pardon for our failures to live out the life given in Baptism. Now we need to learn yet more how to live our Christ-life, to learn from the total scriptural experience of those who responded to God's call and to apply this experience to our own day-to-day life. Now we are ready to pray for each other's needs and the whole work of the Church in today's world. This is the total context in which we grow in our ability to unite ourselves to the self-offering of Christ.

Learning to Celebrate

60. This is the framework in which the adult works as he shares his own eucharistic life with the child. Gradually, over the years of childhood his own more mature understanding will be shared, but only in such measure as the child's spiritual growth allows. As a first communicant, it is adequate for him to know that we are being invited, as members of God's family, to share in the sacred meal in which Jesus gives us himself, but even by the time he enters adolescence, because of limited experience, he is not yet ready for the full scriptural idea of sacrifice. We aim, during middle and later childhood, to enable children to make each Mass a true celebration of joy and thanksgiving for the present living of baptismal life.

This learning is best done with practice. The good syllabus will underpin the teaching of home and school, for there are points where it is suggested that a class or group Mass is virtually essential, where a "celebration" of the new realisation of a life situation seems to demand that it be in the Mass. This is not a rival for the Sunday family eucharistic celebration, but a teaching situation, the culmination of an area of work. Never, of course, should it be allowed to be only this.[5] That is why such celebration cannot be just *ad hoc.* Time must be spent in preparation and all concerned must be involved, the celebrant being invited from the start, so that he can be fully aware of the children's needs.[6]

Exploring Eucharistic Symbolism

61. All during this period, as already suggested, projects on the symbols of bread, wine and meal will have shown the child that bread, a staple food, is the work of many hands and therefore, represents man, as wine represents his joy. Until this is understood, the idea may need to be expressed explicitly by taking to the altar some actual "work of his hands".

Thinking about birthday parties, Christmas dinners, and other celebrations will have helped the child to realise that a communal meal expresses both unity and joy. Stories and poems might have led him on to the particularly Eastern idea of meal whereby a bond is formed with those who have shared one's table. By later childhood he will recognise that food represents life, given and received; that, in fact, we are made out of food: I share food; I share life. Yet food can be harmful. Familiarity with Third World posters and television documentaries will have taught that the starving child cannot immediately digest food, which may even cause death. One needs to be ready for it.[7]

The Symbols in Scripture

62. As with the other sacramental symbolism, simple Bible explorations will have deepened the meaning. The children will have learned of the "bread from heaven", the manna, which sustained the chosen family of God on their journey to freedom. Before "New Covenant" can have meaning, the word itself will have been examined in modern terms and the idea expressed will have become familiar from the stories of Abraham and Moses.

A vivid description of the Passover meal might lead to a celebration in simplest form to make the experience even more memorable. They are too young, as yet, for a formal Passover meal, but the good story-teller will set the scene: the couches round the table prepared with wine, herbs and bread; the lamb, already sacrificed in the Temple, roasting in the oven. Then comes the ceremonial washing of hands before the family take places, reclining round the table. After the first cup of wine, expressing joy in deliverance, the meal begins with hors d'oeuvres, the bitter herbs by which a bitter situation is recalled. Now the real act begins with the father "breaking bread" as he prays a grace of thanksgiving. After the roast lamb and vegetables comes the moment the youngest boy has been waiting for. It is he who asks the ritual question "What is the meaning . . .?" His father's reply is not a fixed formula but always includes recalling the Exodus when their forefathers first ate the sacrificial lamb, after sprinkling the doorposts with its blood. He points out the unleavened bread, denoting haste and the desire to start afresh on a completely new life, the wine expressing joy in new-found freedom. The family rise to join in the Hallel psalm. In this way the children begin to understand that a "memorial" to the Jew made the past present, actualised an event from the past so that it could be shared in the present.

63. Some time later one would draw out the comparison with the Last Supper, now giving fuller meaning to the washing of feet, "he who puts his hand . . .", the discourses, the familiar words: "This is my body which will be given for you"; ("This is really me. I give myself for you"); "This is the cup of my blood" — ("This is my life. I give it up for you"). An older child can be helped to recognise that this is indeed a "New Covenant" because it expresses a new reality; a new value is set on the symbols. Their meaning is raised to a new level, making present at each eucharistic celebration the Passover of Christ: the death, resurrection, ascension of Christ. It is the risen, glorified Christ who is received.

At other times the catechist would enrich the children's background: the wine at Cana, "the first of the signs", or the bread which fed five thousand and, on the next day, the searching test of faith: "Your fathers ate manna in . . . the bread that I shall give . . . this is intolerable language . . . Lord, to whom shall we go?"

Meeting Christ in Joy

64. In all these ways, the children will have been helped to understand that, in the Eucharist, Christ is giving himself to us in love; that our faith and love are pre-supposed when we approach and that, as a result of this union with Christ, our faith and love are intensified. (This could be compared with ordinary human relationships where love given occasions a loving response.) We eat and we take Christ with us out into the world: "Go in peace to love and serve the Lord". The serious risk is that all could remain at the knowledge level, just an intellectual exercise, unless we help the children to interiorise a response. This is the food of life. Christ lives in me that I might live in him — NOW, as a child, as well as in the future. This meal unites me to Christ and to the Church — and this means people. The more I receive this food the more I must try to conform myself to the mind and will of Christ, "Imitate what you handle" the priest is told at ordination. The injunction applies to us, too. At each stage of learning we must pause and allow the children to ponder. Perhaps we could prepare with a group a simple Bible vigil or celebration. Certainly we should use the feastdays, especially Corpus Christi, and the eucharistic liturgy itself. We cannot profitably teach the Eucharist unless with the intention of leading to a fuller appreciation which "is intended to help children to meet Christ with joy in the celebration of the Eucharist and to stand with him in the Father's presence".[8]

FURTHER REFERENCE:

DCM;
GCD 58;
TFNW 32, 46, 72, 73, 87, 114, 115.

USEFUL FOR PARENTS AND TEACHERS

Celebrating Mass with Children, Matthews, Collins;
Children Give Thanks, Matthews, Collins;
We Celebrate the Eucharist, Brusselmans;
Children's Mass Book, Richardson, Mayhew-McCrimmon;
At Home with God, BRES (many sections).

NOTES:

[1] DCM 6
[2] DCM 8
[3] DCM 2
[4] Jn 15:13
[5] DCM 13 and "Cornerstone" 160
[6] DCM 23
[7] Cf. Jn 13:1-15 and 1 Cor 11:17-29
[8] DCM 55

7.

Helping Children to Live in the Church

(cf. Cornerstone 51a; 58b; 63; 95-107; 180; 190; 204a-c; 218; 220)

The Infant in the Church: The Domestic Church

65. "The promotion of the spiritual growth of believers means introducing them ever more fully into the life of the Church . . . To form a christian mentality means to nourish that sense of belonging to Christ in the Church".[1] In childhood this is truly a matter of nourishment, rather than of direct teaching. The total environment, including most especially the example and attitudes of the adults predominant in this environment, the general catechesis and sacramental formation are the means whereby the child becomes aware of what it is to be a member of the Church, the mystical body of Christ, in the world of today. A child learns how to live his family life because his living of it is nurtured by his family. This is part of the tragedy of an unhappy childhood, that it tends to have its repercussions for generations to come.[2] A child learns his native language years before he knows which is his native land. Later he will go to school and learn it more formally, learn its structure and the possibilities of great beauty in its use.

Here we have a very close parallel with the way in which a child learns how to live as a member of the Church, learns its language of prayer and liturgy. For most children, it will be in later childhood that we begin any formal teaching on the Church. From babyhood they will have been practising their membership and learning to speak its language for "it is through the family that they are gradually initiated into association with their fellowmen in civil life and as members of the people of God".[3] That is why Vatican II speaks of the family as "the domestic Church".[4] The fortunate tiny Christian first learns from the loving care of his parents that the purpose of authority is service.[5] It is from the care and concern shown by older members of the family for elderly or sick neighbours that he internalises the meaning of christian love, long before he could possibly express it in words.[6] Well before he can understand their particular function, his father's work in the SVP, his mother's devotion to the UCM or his older brother's loyalty to the YCW will have taught him that particular forms of service can be expressed in Church societies.

As he attends Mass with his family, shares in the joy of the first Communion of an older brother or sister, or watches the new baby being baptised, he begins to feel rather than understand the meaning of communal worship. The child nurtured in a truly christian family senses that belonging to the Body of Christ is a total commitment, not simply a Sunday duty, and this years before anyone has taught him that: "the Church is the community of those who love one another with one Spirit and who persevere in the teaching of the apostles in fraternal union, in the breaking of bread and in prayers[7] . . . in the determination to build on earth the family of God, in truth, in justice and in hope".[8]

The Second Christian Community: School

66. It is perhaps his first experience of a family baptism that will teach a child that he belongs to the family of God as well as to his own family. Certainly he is ready to be made aware of this when he has settled at school and realises that here is another community to which he belongs. If his school is truly a christian community[9] it will become for the child a microcosm of the Church, an extension of the family-Church which has been his first "educator". Here he can be educated to appreciate that he is "precious" as a "living stone" in the fabric of the Church.[10]

Helping the Child of the non-practising Family

67. It is in this area, of course, that the school meets the major problem. The teacher may be a committed Catholic, well-skilled professionally and a trained catechist, but even in the earliest stages of the primary school, he will have difficulty in meeting the very mixed needs of the children in his care. Even the least experienced class-teacher becomes quickly aware of the varying degrees of commitment to the Church of the families to which his pupils belong. The parents of one child may be fully active and committed, those of another, non-practising, whose relationship with the Church is tenuous and there will be all stages in between.[11] Just as there will never be the perfect family-Church, so there will not be the perfect school community Church. Perhaps this is only to admit the reality of Chapter 7 of the Dogmatic Constitution on the Church where we are reminded that, although called to holiness, we are still the Pilgrim Church. Rather than be disheartened, the teacher will use his expertise to encourage the fortunate child and in some way heal or supply what is lacking in the home of his fellow-pupil. Becoming involved, under the guidance of a thoughtful committed teacher, in class prayers and celebrations, as well as school assemblies, can in some measure, help the child to fathom the meaning and value of communal prayer and worship which otherwise he might not experience.

The local parish community can be of immense service here. Not only can it make a full response to the urgent request of the 1977 Synod of Bishops for effective adult catechesis, but also support in every way the catechetical effort of the school, especially by helping, in the case of those affected by religious indifference, "to establish contact with the families . . . so that some means can be found to open a dialogue with them".[12]

First Experiences of God's Family

68. In the early years in school the teaching will be indirect and what the child gathers about the Church will be the result of the experiences deliberately structured by the teacher, as well as the total experience of belonging to a larger "community of faith".[13] He will learn that he belongs to God's family, because he has been chosen by Baptism when he was first taken to Church as a tiny baby that this belonging is a happy experience; that we all help to spread this happiness, but that we can spoil it. Because God loves us all so much, Jesus came to tell us about his Father. Jesus taught his friends how to live as friends of God. He is alive today and helps us, in God's big family, to love and praise his Father with him.

Learning to be a Child in the Church

69. In middle childhood, the concepts of the Church which are given will still be focused on the child himself. It is because Jesus has shown us the way to his Father that we learn how to live his new life for by now the child is beginning to realise that the Church is people, not a building. Yet he will respect that building and behave with reverence within it, for it is here that "God dwells with men" and here too that the local Church gathers to worship God as a parish community. As he explored the parish church with parent or teacher, its furnishings will have told their "story" and so have provided him with concrete background for ideas of liturgy and tradition learned elsewhere. The child now learns how special friends of God have accepted his invitation to belong to his Church-family. By finding out what they did, he discovers how we today can do the same. Carefully prepared class Masses will enable the members of a class group to experience eucharistic worship especially geared to their needs, so they are initiated into the "sign-language" of the Church. Theme-work on the signs of Pentecost and vivid stories of how the Apostles were transformed by the action of the Holy Spirit, will provide a vicarious experience and so stimulate a personal response from each child.

Preparation for Commitment

70. It is in the years of later childhood that more formal teaching will begin. Now the child is capable of some understanding of symbolism. A simple study of the liturgy of Baptism will help him to appreciate not only that it is by this sacrament that we are incorporated into the Church, but also the effects of such membership. This will be continued as he learns something of the mystical body and of how those who lived as model Christians, help us similarly to build up today's Church, for now he begins to recognise that we are all the Church, not just the bishops, priests and religious, that each of us contributes to the health of the whole organism.[14] Now the Bible is presented as the book of the Church. Particularly around Christmas time, by some practical project, he will be initiated into the meaning of christian service. By exploring the symbolism of bread and meal a deeper understanding will be given of the Eucharist as the communal worship of the Church.

Probably only in the final year in the primary school will some attempt be made to introduce the hierarchical structure of the Church by showing the relationship of service within it, as similar to the relationships within the child's own family. In this way, he will discover the Church in action in the world of today, gain some idea of the complementary function of the Pope, bishops, priests, religious and laity and become aware of the missionary activity of the Church.

Openness to Ecumenism

71. There cannot be any attempt to explain ecumenism, but there is great need to foster an ecumenical spirit. This is particularly so when many children have one parent who is a non-Catholic Christian. Sensitive teaching will certainly help the child to live more happily in his family.

Openness to the World

72. If the school is situated in a multi-cultural area, it is essential that throughout childhood a respect for the religions of others will have been fostered. Now in later childhood, attempts will be made, probably mainly through personal contacts, to teach that other children worship God in different ways, that we respect them and pray for them.

A Child's Concept of the Church

73. By the end of childhood the basic concepts necessary for an understanding of the Church will have been acquired: the Church is God's family to which we are privileged to belong because of our baptism; the Church is the Body of Christ acting in the world of today; meetings with Christ in the Church (particularly Eucharist and other sacraments) strengthen our commitment; our worth to the Church is expressed by our response, as an individual or as members of the whole group; the Church has a hierarchical structure that service may the more readily meet men's needs. Whether these concepts remain as intellectual ideas or become active in the child's spiritual life will be dependent upon his actual experience of the living Church, at home, in school and in his parish for "the child has a right to the love and help of the community".[15] Commenting on this, Mark Searle adds:

"In asking to have their child baptised, parents explicitly undertake to do their best to bring their child up on the christian way of life. But it is also true . . . that the Church has responsibility for those it baptises and . . . it is the local Church or parish which implicitly accepts that responsibility and undertakes to assist the parents in their difficult and delicate task. It is for this reason that Catholic schools exist . . . In the future, as in the past, the religious formation of the child we baptise will be the shared responsibility of both the Catholic family and the wider christian community".[16]

FURTHER REFERENCE:

GCD 65-67;
TFNW 42-55; 86-89; 142-144; 151-152; 154-156; 182-184;
CT 10-13; 24; 32-34; 47; 67.

PARENTS AND TEACHERS WILL FIND USEFUL:

Christening, The Making of Christians, Mark Searle, OFM, (Kevin Mayhew).

NOTES:

1 TFNW 42-43
2 Cf. *Cycles of Affirmation,* J. Dominian, Darton, Longman & Todd
3 DCE 3
4 DCC 11
5 Jn 13:14-15
6 Jm 2:15-17
7 Ac 2:42
8 TFNW 47
9 Cornerstone 218
10 Cf. 1 Pet 2:4-5
11 Cf. Cornerstone 219
12 GCD 81
13 Cornerstone 218
14 1 Cor 12:12-27
15 Rite of Baptism for Children, n. 4
16 *Christening, The Making of Christians,* p. 51

8.

Doctrine and Children

(cf. Cornerstone 140-154)

Necessity for Doctrine

74. In presenting the fruits of the fourth Synod of Bishops (October, 1977), Pope John Paul II commends all the four "great ways" of religious education to catechists: scripture, doctrine, liturgy and life-experience, re-affirming the principles of the *General Catechetical Directory* and subsequent documents. Placing catechesis in the framework of the Church's pastoral and missionary activity, he defines it as "an education of young people and adults in the faith, which includes especially the teaching of christian doctrine imparted, generally speaking, in an organic and systematic way, with a view to initiating the hearers into the fullness of christian life".[1] Much later on, when considering the joy that faith can bring amidst the difficulties of modern living, he advocates clear, positive guidance for the young. "When educating children . . . let us not give them too negative an idea of faith . . . let us show them that the humble yet courageous seeking of the believer . . . is based on the word of God who cannot deceive or be deceived . . . It is also one of the aims of catechesis to give to young catechumens the simple but solid certainties that will help them to seek to know the Lord more and better".[2]

This confirms the teaching of the Bishops of England and Wales that "catechesis is a teaching, a clear and increasingly profound unfolding of revealed doctrine, which must remain sensitive to the needs and capacities of the faithful".[3] This need for the catechist to receive his own sound doctrinal formation and to be sure of the doctrine he is teaching, while paying due regard to the immaturity of children, is stated again in the very next paragraph where the catechists themselves are reminded that "Above all they are to see that revealed doctrine becomes the fundamental value and inspiration of the whole of christian life".[4] Later, a warning is added: "The educator of faith should . . . understand the complex meaning of his action as a whole . . . if he does use doctrinal terminology and formulas, he should not do so to avoid life, but only to interpret it with greater clarity and authority in the light of faith".[5] Yet the positive value of formulations of doctrine is emphasised again by the Bishops towards the end of the document where they are considering catechetical method: "Doctrinal formulas have an important part to play in the method of catechesis since they do have a considerable pedagogical value . . . (They) present the faith to the human mind in a way which is at once authoritative, illuminating and stimulating . . . They help us in our dialogue with God and with each other, and can lead us to prayer".[6]

Educational Value

75. It is this educational value of doctrine which the Pope takes up again in *Catechesis in Our Time* when defining the special characteristics of catechesis at the different stages of life, from infancy to old age. He speaks of the catechesis of childhood as "the moment for a catechesis aimed at inserting him or her organically into the life or the Church, a moment that includes an immediate preparation for the celebration of sacraments. This catechesis is didactic in character, but it is directed towards the giving of witness in the faith. It is an initial catechesis, but not a fragmentary one, since it will have to reveal, although in an elementary way, all the principal mysteries of faith and their effects on the child's moral and religious life. It is a catechesis that gives meaning to the sacraments, but at the same time it receives from the experience of the sacraments a living dimension that keeps it from remaining merely doctrinal".[7] At a later point when arguing the perennial value of memorisation and advocating its use "in an intelligent and even an original way in catechesis" he proffers suggestions for suitable subjects, but not before he, too, has warned against "reducing all knowledge to formulas that are repeated without being properly understood".[8]

Application to the Adult

76. When we apply these clear principles to the practical situation, whether of the school, the family or the parish, certain points become self-evident. The adult concerned needs personal formation so that his own understanding of doctrine enables him to play his part in catechesis which "should contribute to the gradual grasping of the whole truth about the divine plan".[9] He needs to recognise the limitations of childhood, before the capability of abstract thought has been attained. A syllabus or scheme of work will be constructed upon a concentric plan, so that each year the child is presented with the whole christian message in a manner suited to his present stage of intellectual development yet with deepening appreciation of the mysteries at each stage of growth.

Avoidance of Verbalism

77. Doctrinal formulations suitable and useful for adults will have little meaning for the child and, whilst it is perfectly possible to "teach" them and for the child to commit them to memory, the result is likely to be mere verbalism which may serve as a blockage both to present and future understanding. Even so, as learning proceeds, the child should be helped to formulate what he knows in appropriate language and to memorise the simple statement. Doctrine is not the only, nor even the first "language of faith". Still, as time goes on, it is a language which becomes increasingly important. Knowledge and understanding are not everything. But they have an indispensable part to play in the growth of faith towards maturity.

Doctrine and Prayer

78. Frequently, this will lead to a response in prayer. As the child becomes familiar with the Nicene or other credal formulas in liturgy, phrases can be given meaning at a suitable point in teaching or at an appropriate liturgical season. This vital connection between doctrinal teaching and prayer is emphasised for teachers by Fr Jungmann: "If in catechesis we advance from teaching to prayer, we shall have accomplished the task for which we were appointed. We shall have done what St Augustine wanted us to do — to teach in such a way as to guide the listener from hearing to believing, from believing to hope, and from hope to charity. Faith, hope and charity are not so much special topics of catechesis, but aims towards which every catechesis should strive to attain. They represent spiritual attitudes which ought to result from the sum of our catechetical efforts".[10]

Growing Towards an Expression of Living Faith

79. Over the years, these gradually developing statements will fix his doctrinal knowledge in the child's mind and help him to recall the real religious experiences out of which they were formed. Several of the new syllabuses and the work-books which are developing from them suggest such formulas as the doctrinal expression of each completed theme.[11]

These simple statements which encapsulate real knowledge enable the child to grow in his understanding of the mysteries of faith, as the adults who surround him mediate their faith to him. It is from the experience of living the life of faith as a child that it becomes possible later, during adolescence, when the stage of abstract thinking is reached, to understand and appreciate doctrine.

As a child, his living faith is experienced through meeting Christ in his word in Scripture and celebrating the mysteries in each succeeding liturgical year, so that in time he can begin to penetrate the mystery of the Incarnation and the Paschal mystery, which much later on he will express in doctrinal formulas. His faith is experienced in prayer and in sacramental life expressed in a liturgy in which he can participate.[12] Later he will appreciate the richness of sacramental doctrine. Through living his childhood as a member of his Catholic family, his local parish and his Catholic school, he can later reach an understanding of the doctrinal meaning of Church. So throughout childhood he is absorbing doctrine, learning doctrines, but never in isolation, always as part of a total learning process. He is able to express what he knows in a manner true to his present stage of spiritual development. Verbalism is avoided and the expression fixes his knowledge, becoming an aid to further learning.

FURTHER REFERENCES:

GCD 22-24; 30; 34; 38-39; 63; 47-69; 73;

TFNW 39-40; 54; 85; 177; 189;

CT 20-21; 26-31; 59-61.

NOTES:

[1] CT 18
[2] Ibid 60
[3] TFNW 39
[4] Ibid 40
[5] Ibid 54
[6] Ibid 177
[7] CT 37
[8] Ibid 55
[9] GCD 24
[10] *Handing on the Faith,* p. 262
[11] Cf. *Living and Believing,* (New and Revised Edition), G. O'Mahony, SJ, St Paul Publications
At Home with God Series, BRES, St Paul Publications
[12] CSL 11 and 14

Conclusion

(cf. Cornerstone 63; 64-88)

80. The catechesis of children was once a comparatively easy task, but the world has changed and the teacher in the Catholic school, even in the Catholic primary school, can no longer be sure that the majority of his pupils are practising, or indeed, wish to be practising their faith, since their environment does not speak to them of Christ, but sets its store almost totally upon material things. Many may teach in areas where catechesis seems impossible, where even the young children are not yet ready for the Good News. Teachers may find it necessary to work from a pre-catechesis where even children "should be often helped to examine the transient interests of the time in order to continue their journey of faith and love".[1] The catechist may need to spend some considerable time preparing the ground so as not to sow the word of God in soil which is not prepared to receive it and so bring it to fruition".[2]

Even children today are more sophisticated, some even cynical. We have all met the eleven-year-old who has seen everything and done everything — even if only on television! The competition is great for their attention, on all sides they are bombarded by the media, surrounded by those — even children who mouth the same platitudes as their parents — who find religion faintly amusing and very outdated. "Sometimes questions are raised about the very possibility and appropriateness of giving them a catechesis",[3] and yet the Directory adds: "Catechesis is certainly not to be omitted for such children".

It takes courage to be a catechist in circumstances like these and yet, perhaps, the very daunting nature of the task may bring its own courage when we remember that at his baptism this child was chosen and afterwards anointed and told that God has "given you a new birth by water and the Holy Spirit". His birthright is being snatched from him. His new life is being smothered. At least we can try, as catechists, to prevent further barriers being erected on the way to possible restoration.

81. The catechist of the child will probably never see his work completed, will never know of his success or failure. He can only be sure that he is trying now, as best as he humanly can, to help the child to respond to the action of the Holy Spirit within him. He can try to set the foundations for future commitment. He will echo the words of St Paul: "I must go through the pain of giving birth to you all over again, until Christ is formed in you".[4] Very probably — and many, many times in his career — like St Paul, he will add: "as it is, I have no idea what to do for the best".[5] On such occasions he should listen again to St Paul and ask God for "all the wisdom and understanding that his Spirit gives"[6] remembering that "there is nothing I cannot master with the help of the One who gives me strength".[7] In times of discouragement, parents and teachers would do well to recall how remarkable is their success. Society is committed to materialism and hedonism; children and young people are bombarded, through highly attractive and effective modern media of communication, with worldly values and yet reach christian commitment. Equally numerous therefore should be the occasions when we rejoice with St Paul: "I thank my God whenever I think of you; and every time I pray for all of you, I pray with joy, remembering how you have helped to spread the Good News from the day you first heard it right up to the present. I am quite certain that the One who began this good work in you will see that it is finished when the Day of Christ Jesus comes".[8]

FURTHER REFERENCES:

TFNW *Introduction for England and Wales,* pp. 6-7;
GCD 2-9;
CT 19; 42; 57; 72.

NOTES:

[1] TFNW 31
[2] Ibid
[3] GCD 81
[4] Gal 4:19
[5] Gal 4:20
[6] Col 1:9-11
[7] Ph 4:13
[8] Phil 1:3-6

GENERAL BIBLIOGRAPHY

A. *DOCUMENTARY RESOURCES*

Teaching the Faith the New Way, Bishops' Conference of England and Wales, St Paul Publications.

Cornerstone: Guidelines for Religious Education I, Nichols, K. F., St Paul Publications.

Orientations: Six Essays on Theology and Education, Nichols, K. F., St Paul Publications.

Catechesis in Our Time, Pope John Paul II, St Paul Publications/CTS.

The Catholic School, Sacred Congregation for Christian Education, CTS.

B. *FOR PARENTS AND TEACHERS*

Parents, Children and God, Bullen A., Fontana.

Celebrating Mass with Children, Matthews E., Collins.

The Forgiveness of Sin, Matthews E., Collins.

Living and Believing (New and Revised edition) O'Mahony G. (ed), St Paul Publications.

Together at Baptism, Payne, Ave Maria Press.

Christening, the Making of Christians, Searle M., Kevin Mayhew.

C. *FOR USE WITH CHILDREN*

At Home with God series (1-6), BRES, St Paul Publications.

To God with Love, BRES, St Paul Publications.

To God with Love and Sorrow, BRES, St Paul Publciations.

We Celebrate the Eucharist, Brusselmans C., Pflaum.

We Celebrate Reconciliation, Brusselmans C., Pflaum.

Listen!, McCallen A. J., Collins.

Praise!, McCallen A. J., Collins.